T0128455

Aurora's Arch

Ava Spraggins

Illustrator: Melissa Hernandez

To order additional copies of this book, contact:
Xlibris
844-714-8691
www.Xlibris.com
Orders@Xlibris.com

ISBN: Softcover   978-1-6698-7663-2
       Hardcover   978-1-6698-7664-9
       EBook   978-1-6698-7662-5

Print information available on the last page

Rev. date: 05/04/2023

Dedication

To my grandfather and editor Noe who taught me the roots of foundations. The true meaning of being passionate and the simplicity of life. Only a few years later, but with you with your legacy I took a chance. To my mentor and angel Judy Martin who taught me the importance of being intellectual and that being brave comes in many forms. To convey emotions freely through books. To my enthusiastic and sharp-witted high school teacher Mrs. Koo who helped me find my voice and indicated life lessons through her chosen works. To others whom I didn't mention, you all have inspired me to lead with fidelity and passion through words and life, THANK YOU.

Noe

You were
You are my mentor
An angel that won't let me fall in a hole
A heart so selfless
A mind so unique
A stare that dashed right through my soul
Patience was your virtue
Desire to learn was your push
A therapist
A father
Judgment was never an option
A mutual person
Spoke his mind, when it was necessary
A believer
Faith
Religion
Karma
Words
Have a great power over us
An associate of wisdom
Nevertheless a beautiful soul

Reminisce That Cold Soul

Let me by start to say I'm not insane
I am nowhere near nor away
I do believe we have come today by fate
No man in his right mind will agree on this taste
I come from a mind of syringes and broken crates
Bring back the day of the Lord who all shall say his name
The day of wealth and grace
It's the time that raves such game
I may have the soul that irks
Presence that is proclaimed to be pneumonitis
Run away
Repudiate on all that can break you
Here me when I speak of my maze
To all there should come their reign
Just be patient with all that comes forth your way
And everything shall be back to its pace.

Five to eight
we are

Shuffling boxes left to right,
Looking for the memoirs of my
of our grandparents
on a mission;
to array the world of their goodbye,
such examples of human
they were
Minute by minute anxiety and despair arise,
Gazing at the picture
Through the lens,
my brother shoots back to the memoirs

Memories that make you laugh and cry of joy
let me print you a story of the occurrence of events,
all leading its own pace
the smell of fresh macaroni and cheese
grilled ribs cooking
Yeah you like food ?
Well I do!
I know I'm exposed, it's what makes life such a risk
I wonder...... do they remember that day?
When I meant the world to them,
discussing over jokes
When will I be able to relive being 9 again?

Preferred vs Posted

A time when East and West collide
A time phase
Germans and Jews allege about a propaganda
"Me in kampf"
a horror in Europe
Germans felt on cloud 9
Hiding was the definition of survival
a politician who called himself a leader
and believed in superiority of race
Jews would appreciate a united dine and wine family meal,
then fame or a close – minded individual
Poland
became a sanctuary for the GERMANS.

Never Gone

His love was like the wind
Blissful, unseen
Enticing
The recall of his bittersweet personality
Made him stand out amongst a crowd.
Where yes caressed my every defect/
When they all play the same game
And that wind still is in graved in your presence.
It's something deeper than anything else.
Bittersweet
Masculine
Seductive
A person that made me question empowering
Loses me within reality
You never knew till it was gone,

"is time, suppose to heal?"
Hello?
Can you hear me breathing?
I'm a few steps away from you
Trust me
It has never felt like this before.
one difference
is least of my worries by your side.
Much time has passed for me to tell you I'm sorry for everything I've done.
From the other side,
you are my eyes,
you are my ears
brightness turned to joy.
The time doesn't matter, our destination is what matter
Everyday carrying each step, more in depth

Outsider

I live in a life surrounded by lies
I live in a life of secluded tempers
I live in a life of short remorse

With every second, more getting applied,
With every second, faces circling,
Trying to pretend something they are not.
With every second, I realize where honesty beholds.

Living in a world where everyone seems to be nonchalant
but all they want is to
BELONG.
Holding back
Afraid of rejection,
Living in a world of doubt
timorous to show their identity
Society is impactful
But last will remains.
The irony and negativity one feels for them is feeble.
Faith to live in a change world never dies.

Versions

I'm a dreamer,
a believer
A keen individual that glides the ocean.
Maybe a courageous radical activist?
The impossible is a lie. It hardens, discourages you.
From being an inspiration.
Women of many firsts
Women of many rights
The Canary still seen from within planets away
Teachers uniting in many ways
Leading reform in motivating perpetually today.
Goodbye to the Gilded days.
Bonjour to the good days.

Hallo-Scares

Stares that bewitch you
Make you shiver
From head to toe
All you see are
Eyes
BIG
BOLD
MYSTERIOUS
What may it be?
You take....
a walk home
and OUT,
comes your ludicrous
cousin with his joker face, he says;
"How can I help you today?"

Lynx

From the north: an old lady named Lynx
Who liked to chase lattes.
She said to her friends, exercise was a fun time and with a smile.
She didn't think the same, when she saw a wild cat coming up in the mile.
Now Lynx would be lucky enough to ever see Mr. Binks.

Awaken in the Morning

I dislike waking up
Early in the morning,
Causing a big commotion
Loosing cautiousness
Of my focused dream
Because of one's impertinences.
The fussing sound
One hears repeatedly is such insolence.
One is impotent to keep on dreaming,
In order for no scheme to be caused.
One vibrates
When hearing a whisper
going away for a little bit as a mister.

Then coming back and reminding you
"it's time to get up"
I get into a big fuse and start to diffuse.
Start to visualize it's a sign,
so open my eyes, and see members clicking.
The ear whisper returns
Confounded I felt
someone beside me was waiting,
I came to my senses
touched the floor,
waking up in a rush isn't my favorite.

Survival

Above the frisky views,
dangling from branch to branch
I'm sophisticated and cute
My nuts are hidden in old trees
I remember a young lady starring into the sea
Wearing blue flowy clothes
She carried quarters that called my name
I rushed away
Finally Finally
Found a friend who understood me
Ready Go!
Lunch to eat
Life is beautiful
Experiment with me
A day is never dull
Whirly Twirly
Back to the height I go

The canvas

The years of sword
Cutting of such home
no place, it's enough to hide
soldier up
mountain up to your feet
debts aren't to be paid
in extension
never take what they give
give without expecting
a soldier grows
shocked by the water
is it a fishhook barrel?
seen or unseen dehydration
each breath counted

I can tell how far you've come
never wants to fight anymore
who will throw the first fist?
walk with a slim in dent
he has broken down
contained by the idea it's he, himself only
my friends tell me I'm wrong
every spark of love
comes and goes
never say I didn't tell you
A soldier fears
they too have bones, that don't heal.

Promising like a Mother

Driven like a starfish
Helpless among thee
Might you say bystander?
I may say peace walker!
Conflict vs reality
Intervene roads
Cross paths from a stardust
Come hither under my wing
May your loss cause you righteousness.
May your failures drive you to excel
Pin, pin here we go, may the force stay with thee
"Shirin" like no tomorrow
Promise, like a mother does with her baby.
Chaos may not be an obstacle.

Truth in Denial

Let time be your consultant
You talk with such epistemology
It outstands my era
Your such an ambiguous self being
You erode my certainty to uncertainty
Have we touched that point where limbo is
Our sanctuary?
Let me tell you, I don't care
Let me reframe a thorny rose to thy vigorous mind.
Hope is somewhere 1 to 100.
Waiting for thy charm is like waiting for a caterpillar to bloom.
When all goes wrong remember that I was here to help you through it all.
Never break, keep pushing
You're only a centipede away from the golden line.

Time-lapse

Day and night are our world
Definition of the solar- system
The day can be confusing

Bright buildings that grope the world
Squirrels scattered along the trees, playing tag, hiding their next meal away.

Birds chirping a lullaby, working you up with the happiest of spirits
Hunger on each corner
Hunger to eat
Hunger for knowledge

Sculptured scenery that causes question, then comes night
A language that brings our dreams to reality.

The sound of frogs, and owls
Watching the night away.
Haunting of what is evil
Insomnia mostly practiced
The day lets us dot up all the unseen,
All the foretold, and we begin to appreciate light.

Tied to colonies

Fears take the reins in
Commencement of a late foggy
afternoon in England
Object my riding,
filled astonishment
The Spanish felt terror
All boarded immediately
world spirits
from long thy spoke
My fears moment ten,
Captives divided
Boston
Newport
to every, their deep dejection
I doubted fate!
Overpowered fell the fainted
I recovered from the mistreatment
Was it impossible to dream
Of independence?
Black me believed with such looks
Our time had come
Such portion liquor of red wine seen;
Being Them
My thought wasn't overthrown by
Their feeling
One that broke the barriers was
Our only savior.
Domination would be our future.

Bel homme

You are a unique aurora.
Engrossed my attention the very first time,
sensuality of dangerous lips,
presence of a God

I don't worship you
I just cherish you

Only care,
that has made me feel isolated
and paralyzed
Make me blush like the color of a rose.
You are indefectible in numerous ways .
Fancied me,
As if I was watching a sunset on the ridge
When in reality you have
And are My world.
My actions are of shyness, they are of desirable fear
I can't explain in how many ways you make me feel enormously fortunate.

Gentlemen

Chivalry or courtly love?
Royal status or postal zip code?
A Lord seen
A lawyer unseen
Choose a manuscript or a rusty book?
A male whom is so clever,
Aggressive with his one self,
Would you rather see him in a
girdle
Or a surcoat?

Reeducate

I hate the way one is brainwashed nowadays
It's common way of many race, genders
Making us feel weird to their convenience
The irony of one manipulation is a disgrace
One makes arrangements towards others ignorance.
Why do thee say;
Having an alliance is way easier than having a state of mind or opinion?
Why do I have to follow their command,
"If you don't agree to do this, we will never speak again."
Aren't I a person of my own demand?
Sarcasm is seen
in hallways
households
friends
Will there ever be honesty, commitment?
I won't listen to his denotation

because I want to show my own demonstration!
You offer subordination and a perfect imagination,
You say "Get excellent grades, we will be a happy family."
Then why do I feel this way?
ALONE
But, hey my gut was telling me otherwise.
Don't ask my resentment, you made me this way!
When one says your "despicable" you change everything that was once said
You show silence
Standing so tall and firm
With the sweetest smile.
Revealing to us we weren't deranged after all,
Showing us we were blinded by your perfect lies.
I despise
brainwashing shown in everyday lives.

Polar Times

Walking into a clear state
Authority above
showers us
in success
with abundance
a leaf's tears are frozen,
and instantly lead us to believe,
time is a *clock stopper*.
A window's interior is wood, turning to frost by the second.
Smoke from the chimneys are leveled to 100%,
a picture of hot coco becomes heaven.
On my porch
my dog barks above
feared and confused
sharply icicles reach out.
Every night in some strange house
There are a group of beautiful souls singing in choir.
the manner of a fuzzy hat and crazy boots go unnoticed.

Not- A- Dog

I may have claws
My nose smells
I may not see well outside.
my ears wobble when I run
but then there is the heart
one of heart
one of joy
my human is my muse
my partner
I feel the hatred, I feel the eyes.
dinner is my best meal
I am with all my family
they call me Arthur
I like to say, because of the strength and behavior I possess with my tail and smells
of the mighty KING ARTHUR!
when I am cold I am clothed
with some of the warmest clothes.

Phenomenal Woman

Lately I been losing sleep, playing hard
that I can be shown a sign in counting the stars
I see you in my past
Reminiscing like it were years that went by
but can't vision you in my future
Dear, Aura
has it been so long,
that your smooth blue eyes are far too far to remember?
It's late and I been loosing sleep playing on odor street, all you see are
simple roads,
but narrow
Filled with blossoming flowers
on each balcony
that's love
love, she emphasized in your world
are you relaxed?
more like stubborn minds,
fragile hearts,
cold shoulders.

That Laugh

She was giggles
All about making you smile
A passionate soul
A soul seeker
Naïve
Sassy
Intelligent
She proved the definition of great food.
Never a sad time with her
A hunger of adventure
And dreams
Carried her
All she wanted was to love
Giggled a little more
Look into her eyes
Try to win her at a starring contest
Can you testify in coming out alive?
For the good she was, was never enough
She was driven to be the best
Owed it to her loved ones
You say their rare
Glance one more time,
For all you know perfect wasn't perfect anymore

The most imperfect. Hard- headed, mysterious,
and passionate soul
Was along your destiny
Inferiority to pain is not existent
In order to live one must feel pain.
Accept it
Let it be engraved
From the pain
You will rise
Grow tall
Grow wiser
Love deeper
Find the most valuable existence
Is of words, that shouldn't be untold
Let the world understand you
Be an inspiration
Give a hand
lead those that are lost
Never doubt your judgement.

Creatures of the Night

Dear Grandpa,
I wish you can remember ;
the stares that bewitch you
that make you feel safe and at the same time
shiver
Shiver in the excessiveness of the unknown

An owl that tends to lay on the window sill
which shows no signs of danger
because you made it with dedication,
several coats
it's eyes, are composed of dark black wood
it's feathers, well their carved and burned
with a burning pen, and painted with pastel
colors

A present that is ravishing
not because of its price, nor its texture
colors,
a beauty, due to the significance that it
resembles your spirit
A spirit, that was pure
full of serenity and wisdom.
A ravishing piece that will continue to be
passed down in generations to come

A beauty that will refresh my memories as
an infant
It makes me reminisce, of that one time in
my life when i felt completely full and free.
A childhood memory,where we were
dancing windows opened
and a fresh spring dandelion smell, breezed
in. I was dazed,
I was put face to face with my soulmate.

Back to those infant years, when I spotted
the bird's head turn 270 degrees
moment where I presence it stare at me with
those eyes
and something inside of me, screamed
"Please don't leave"
Can you remember when I was distraught,
thinking it was starving,
and I was seconds from approaching it, but
your voice made me STOP?
Yes! The creature of the night
The definition of wisdom, seeker of souls
An owl that seemed to seek your soul,
grandpa

Ever, have you ever, come across this one
thing, creature or person change your life for
the better?
Well, this owl made of your rusty hands
filled with pasture colors
and built with such dedication
is a beauty.
It represents bravery as an infant
curiosity to want to help the unknown

Days go by, and it's just a reflection of the
individual I prosper to be like you grandpa.

Sincerely,
Your granddaughter

Ava Spraggins penned her first poetry when she was fourteen years old, that accompanied by her enthusiasm for oil painting. Her mentors and professors pushed her to keep writing and to enlighten people to distinguish the world's enrichments. A young woman whose grandfather was her mentor and encouraged her to get engaged with the Holocaust Museum to study about essential historical literature from past generations. In continuation her passion for cultures, religions, poetry, and history developed. Transitioning her to start her literary career with a book on how women experience the world through their eyes.

Aurora's Arch is a short story-poetry written with the intention of teaching people about diversity, integrity, humanity, and the manifestation of the good that society desires to see in the world. Cultivating how human experiences affect the world and appreciating such perceptions. Emerging the raw authenticity of how women see the world through their eyes.

Author

Stephanie Cabrera graduated with a Bachelors in English and minor in Political Science. She has been a high school teacher for public schools and boarding schools over the years. Currently is a high school English teacher who specializes in Old English Literature, as well as a member of non-profit organizations for Regent Prep and Stem students. Her research and contributions are geared to assisting others in finding their voice through literacy and writing. She loves to learn and is still in the process of completing another degree, to which she rather stay silent about. One of her hobbies consists of playing piano and appreciating the arts. Throughout her undergraduate career and after college she has always had a passion for law and children, which has led her to engage with several foundations, museums, and the District Attorney's office.

Printed in the United States
by Baker & Taylor Publisher Services